CUTE QUOTES COLORING BOOK

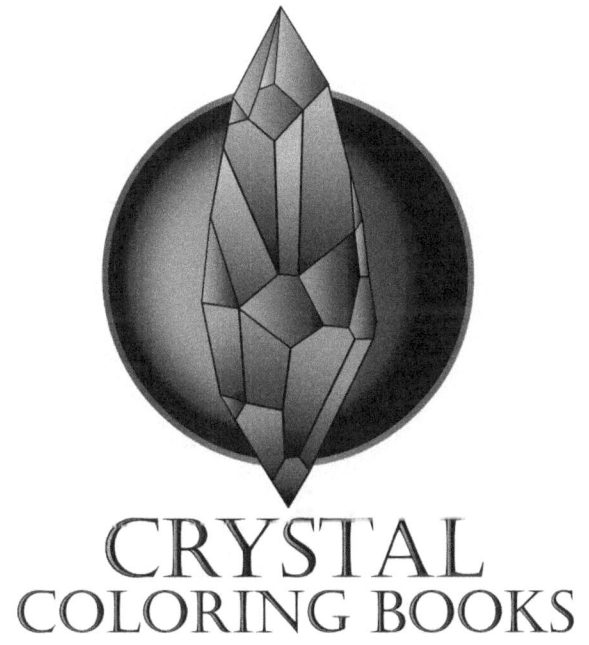

CRYSTAL COLORING BOOKS

Copyright © 2017 Crystal Coloring Books
All rights reserved.
ISBN-13: 978-1979017428
ISBN-10: 1979017425

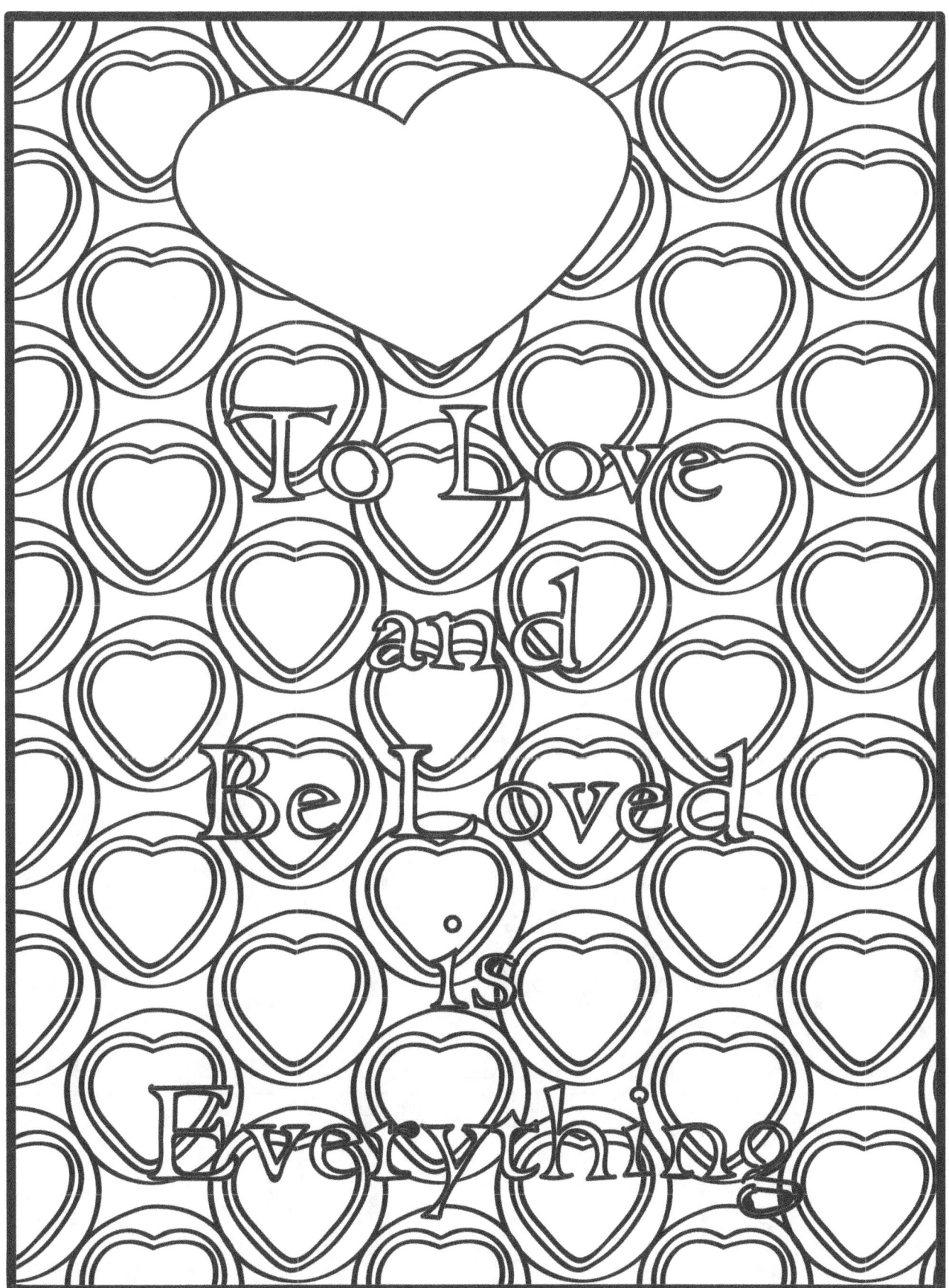

I Choose You

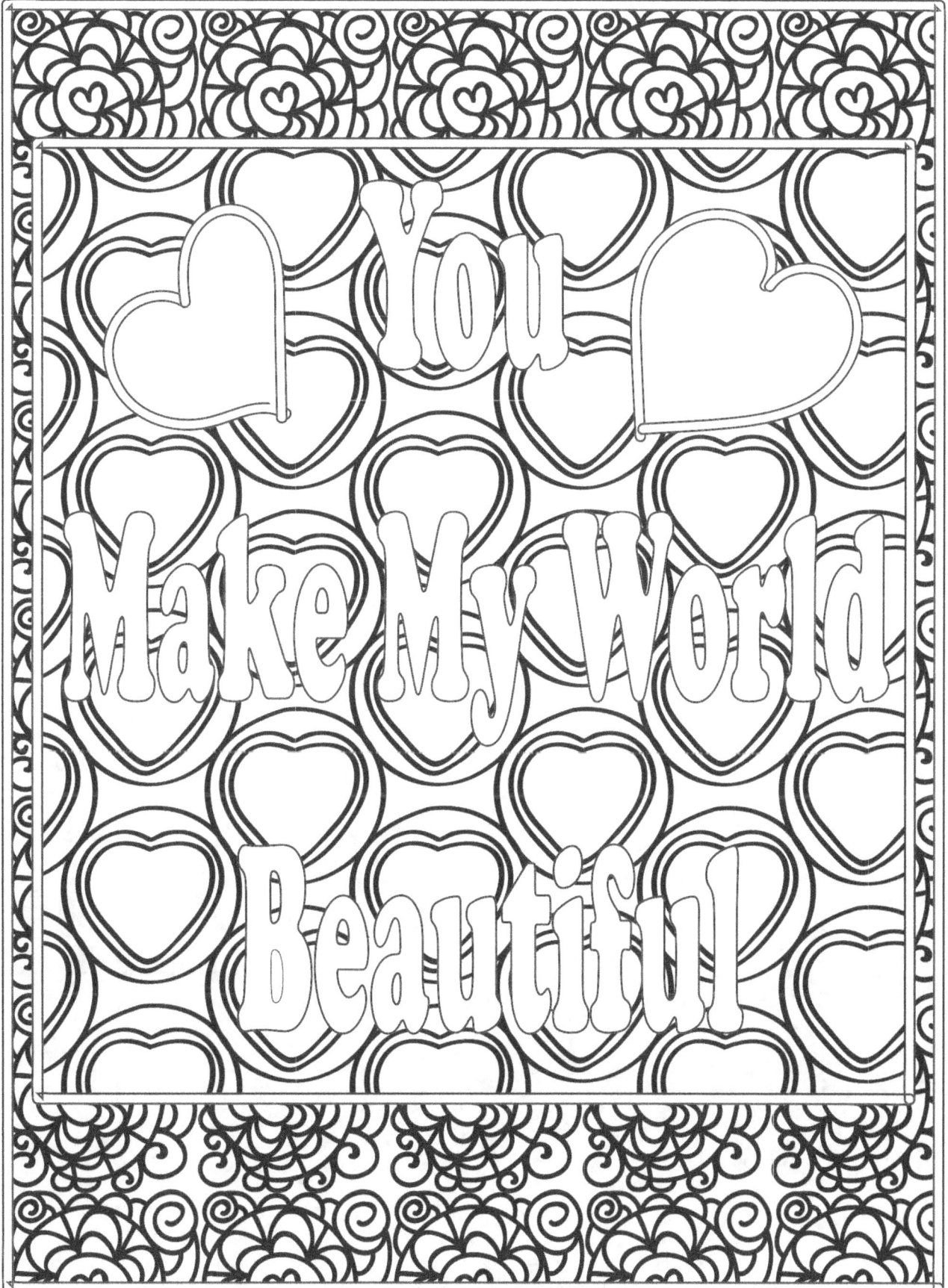

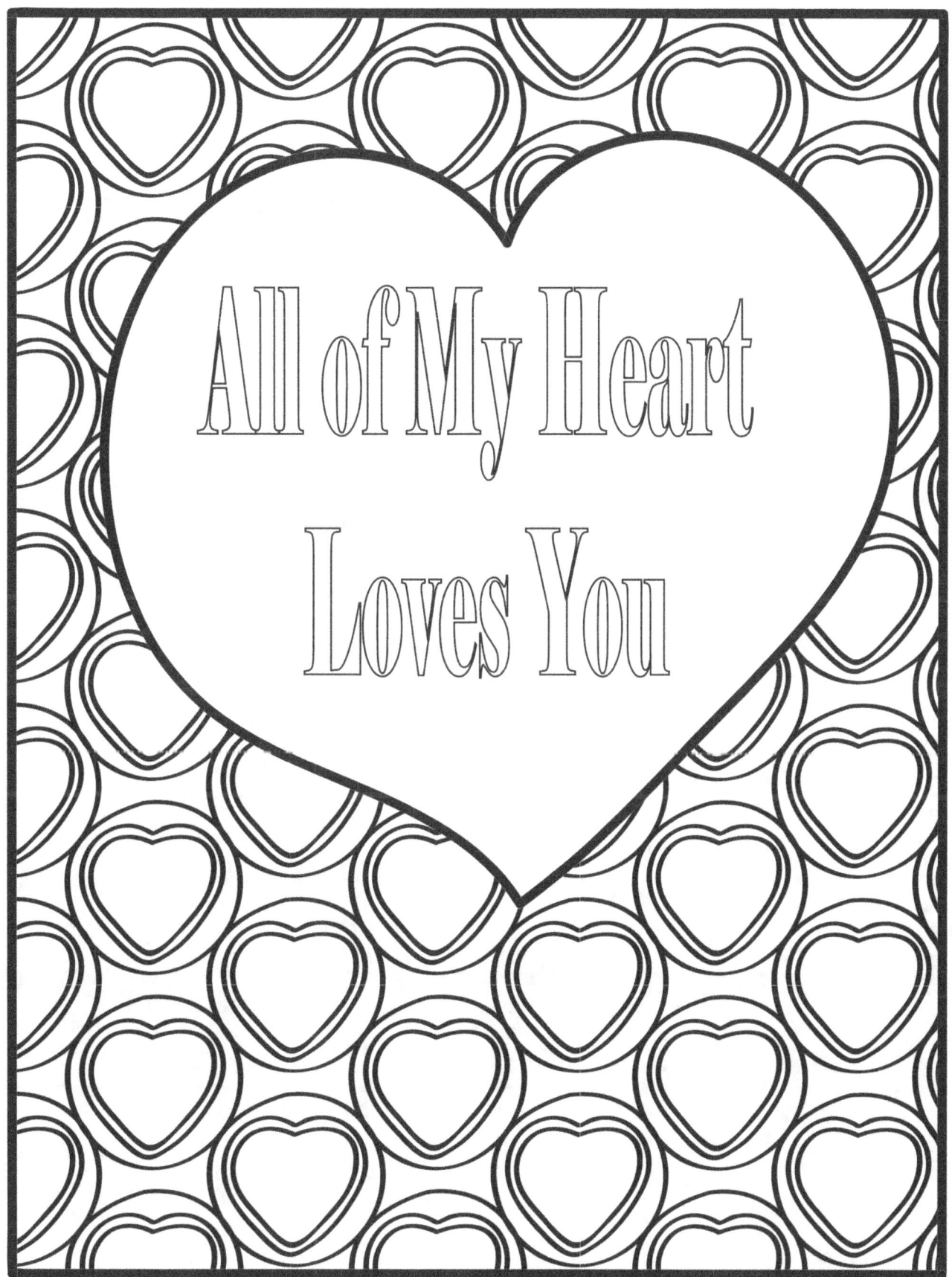

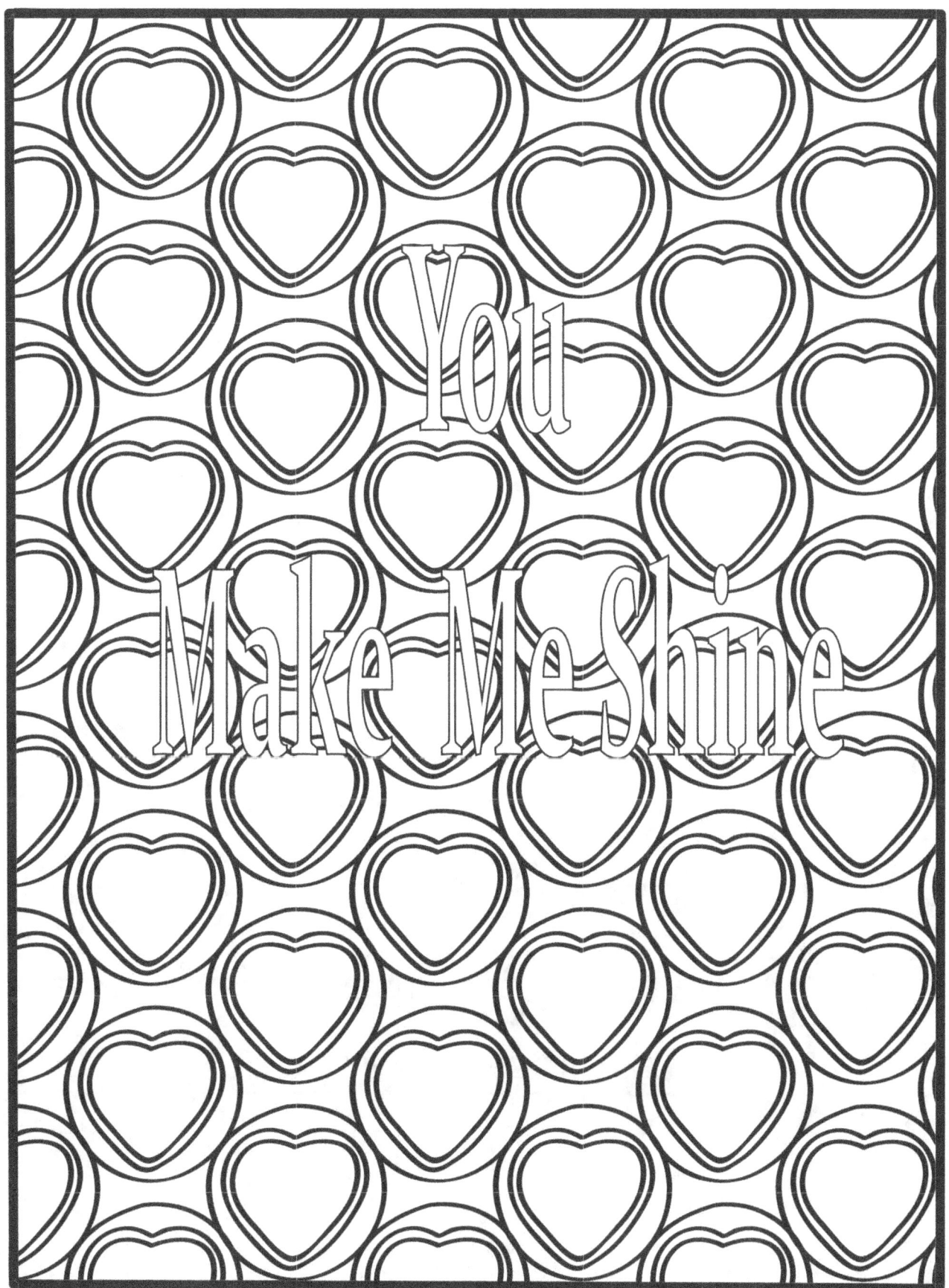

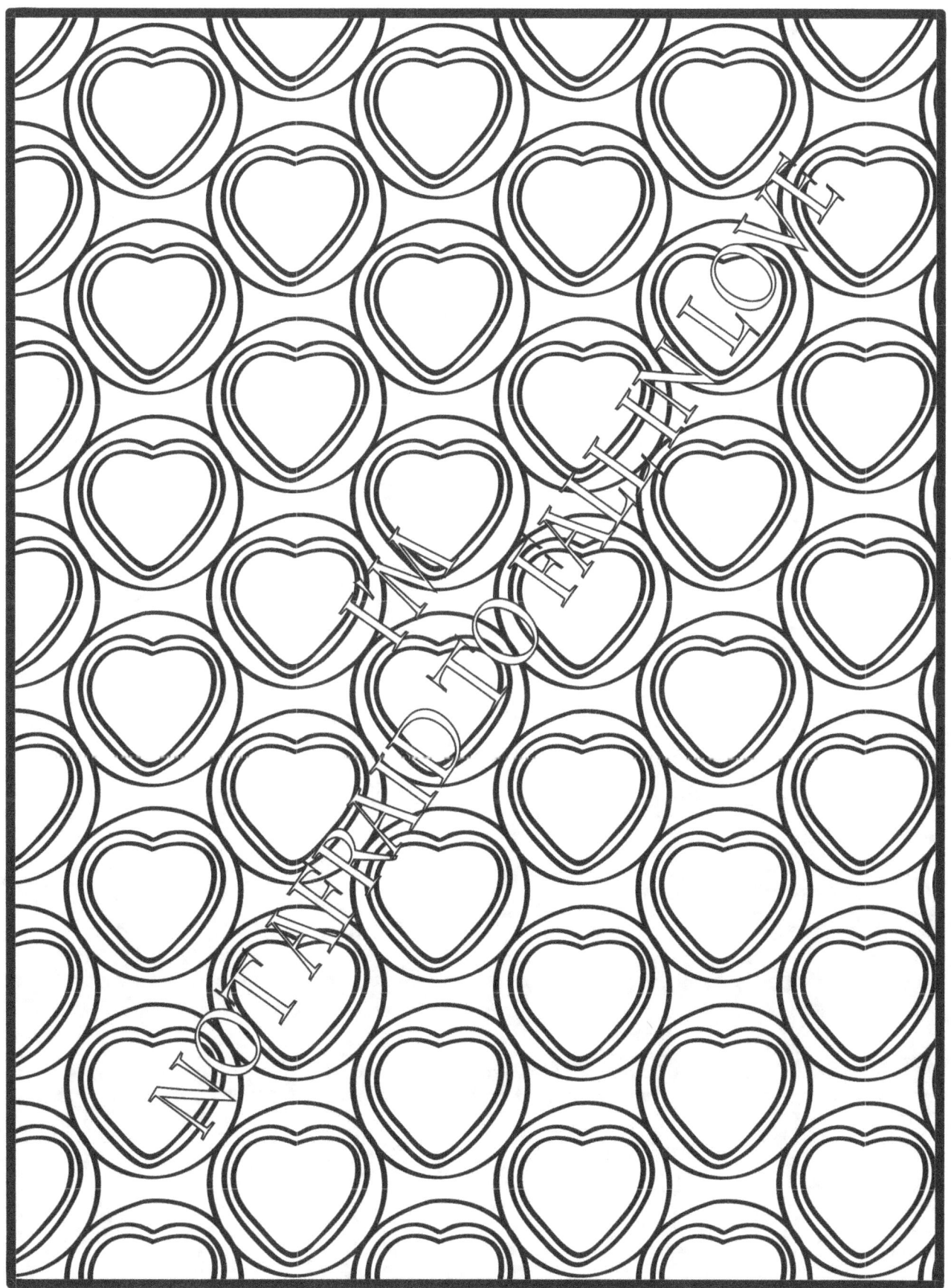

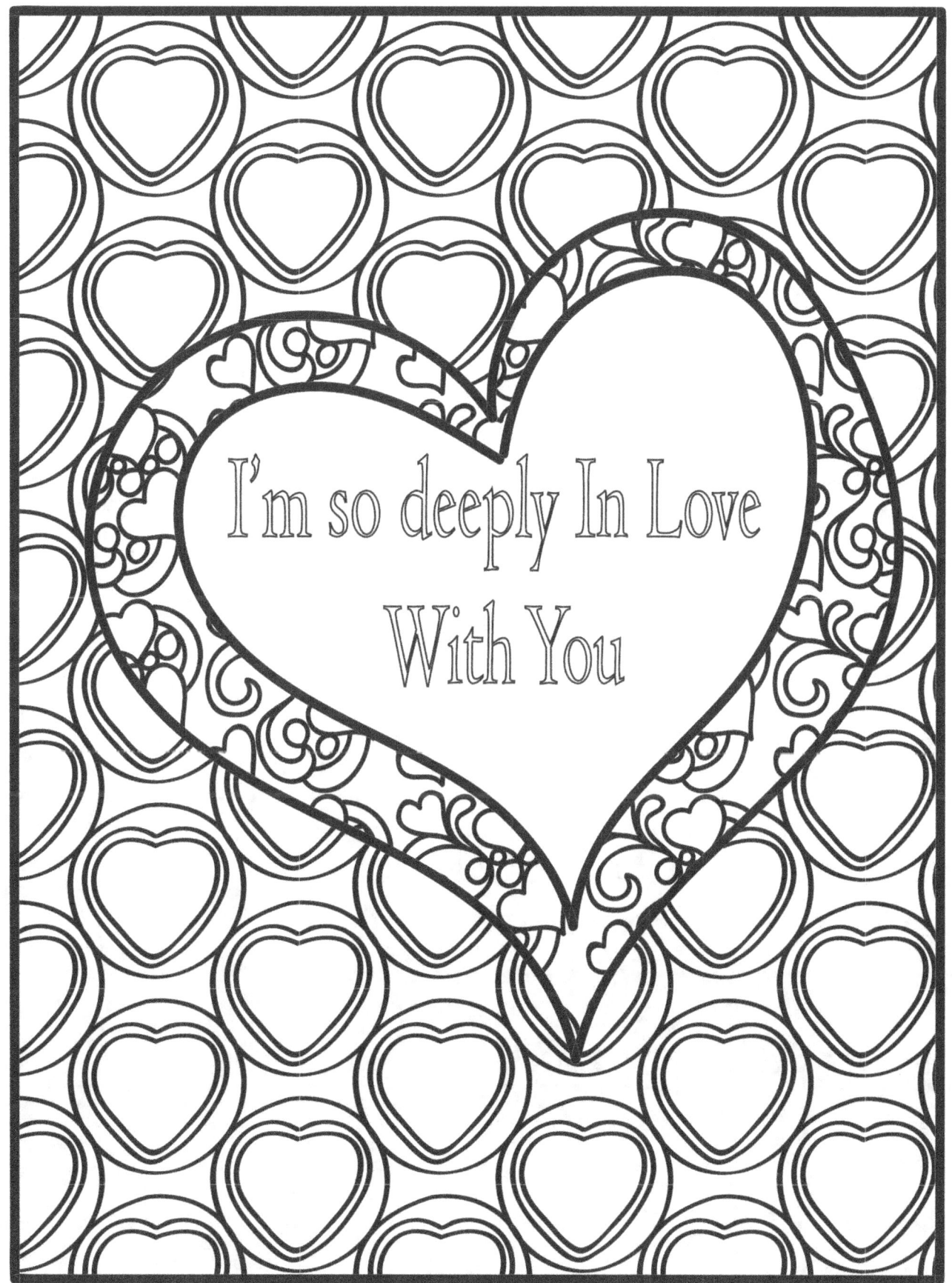

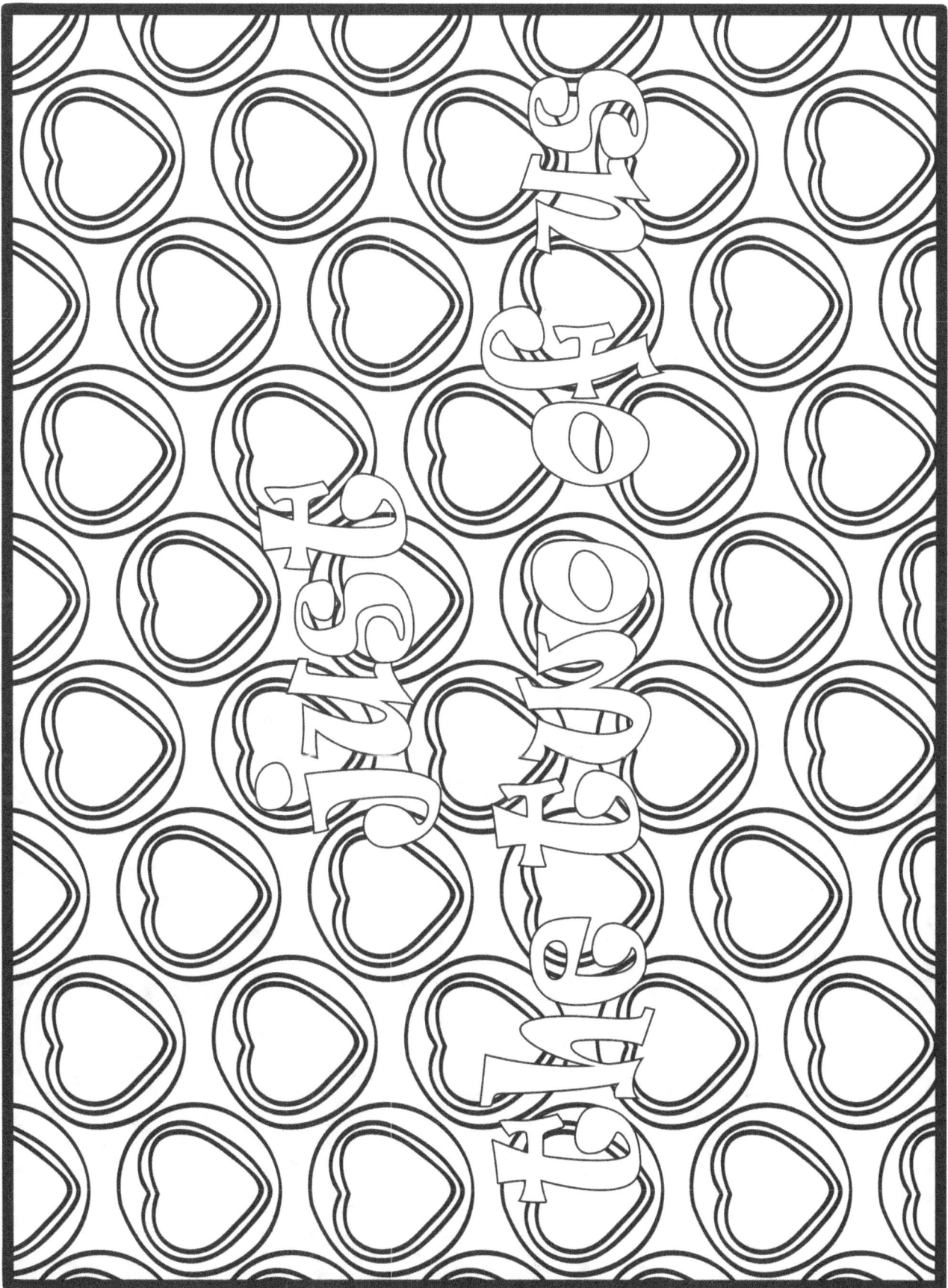

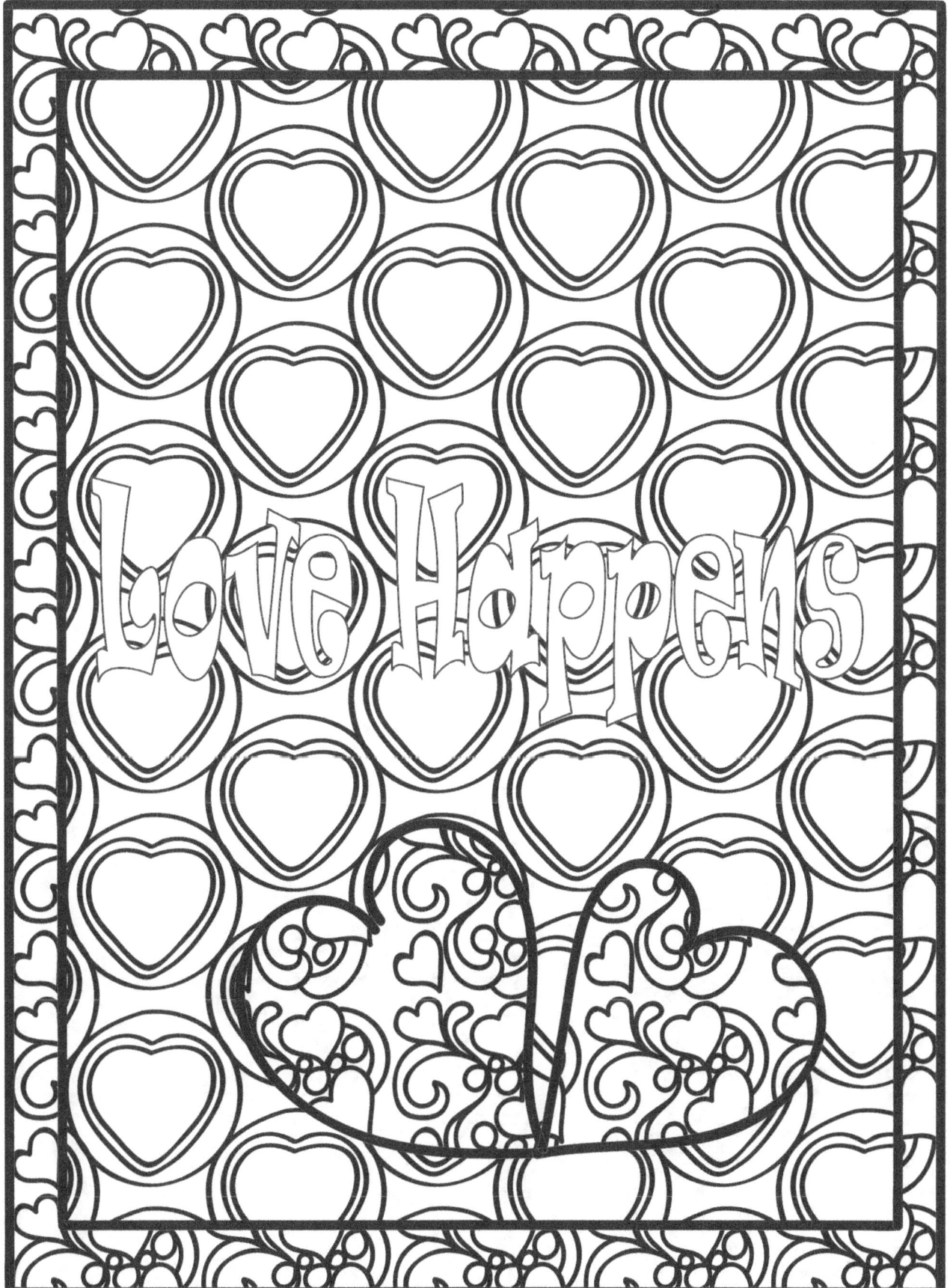

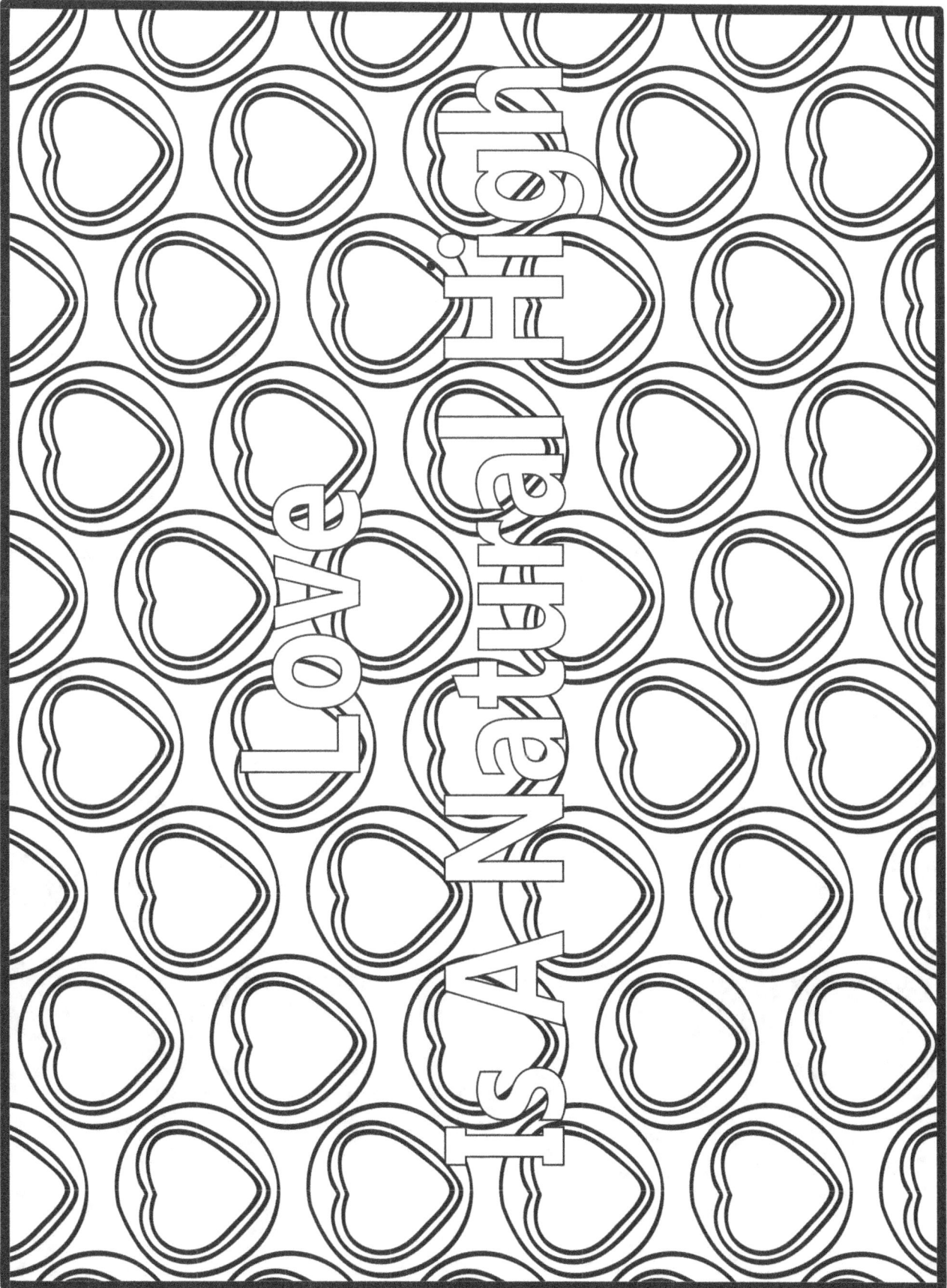

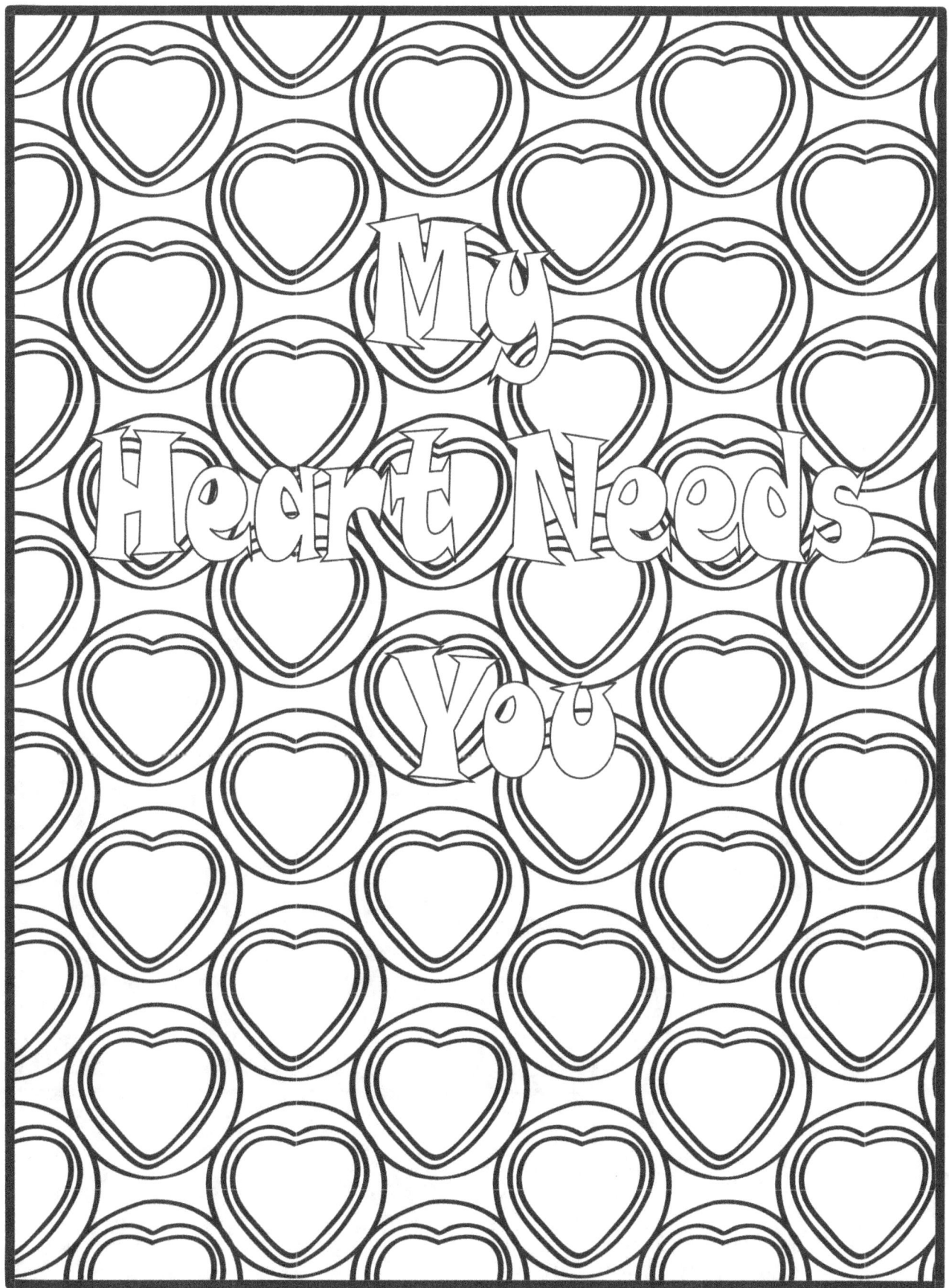

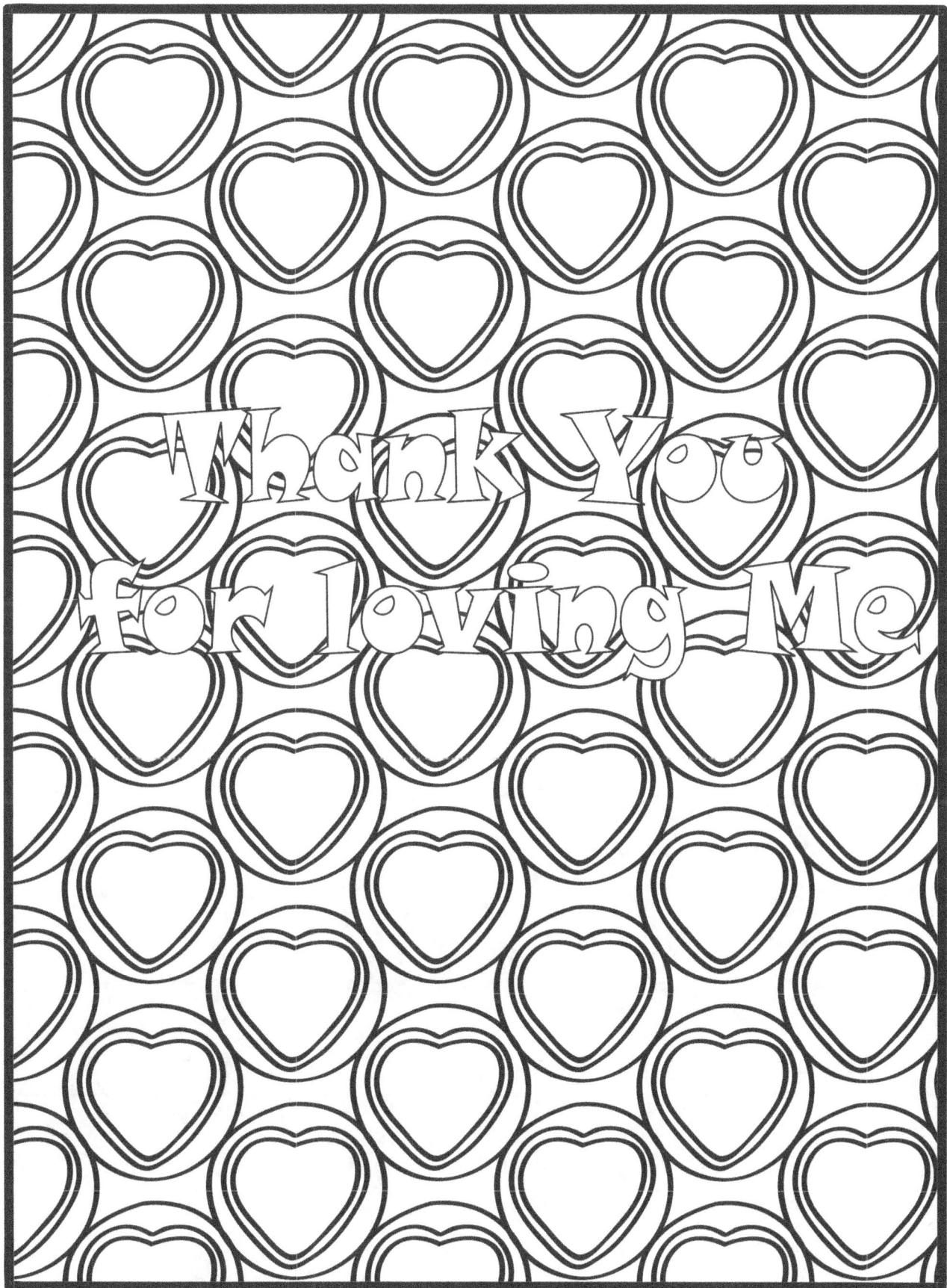

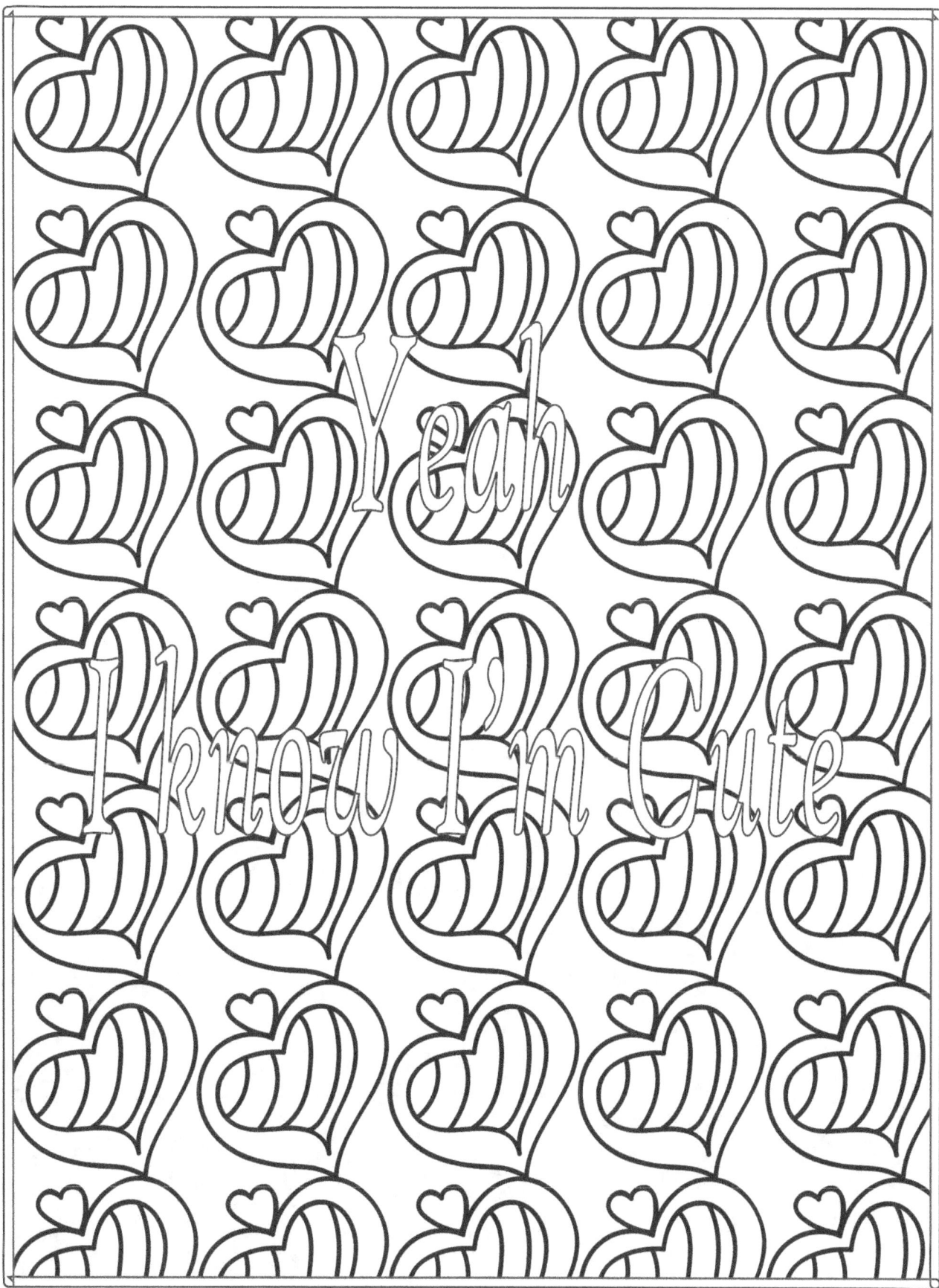

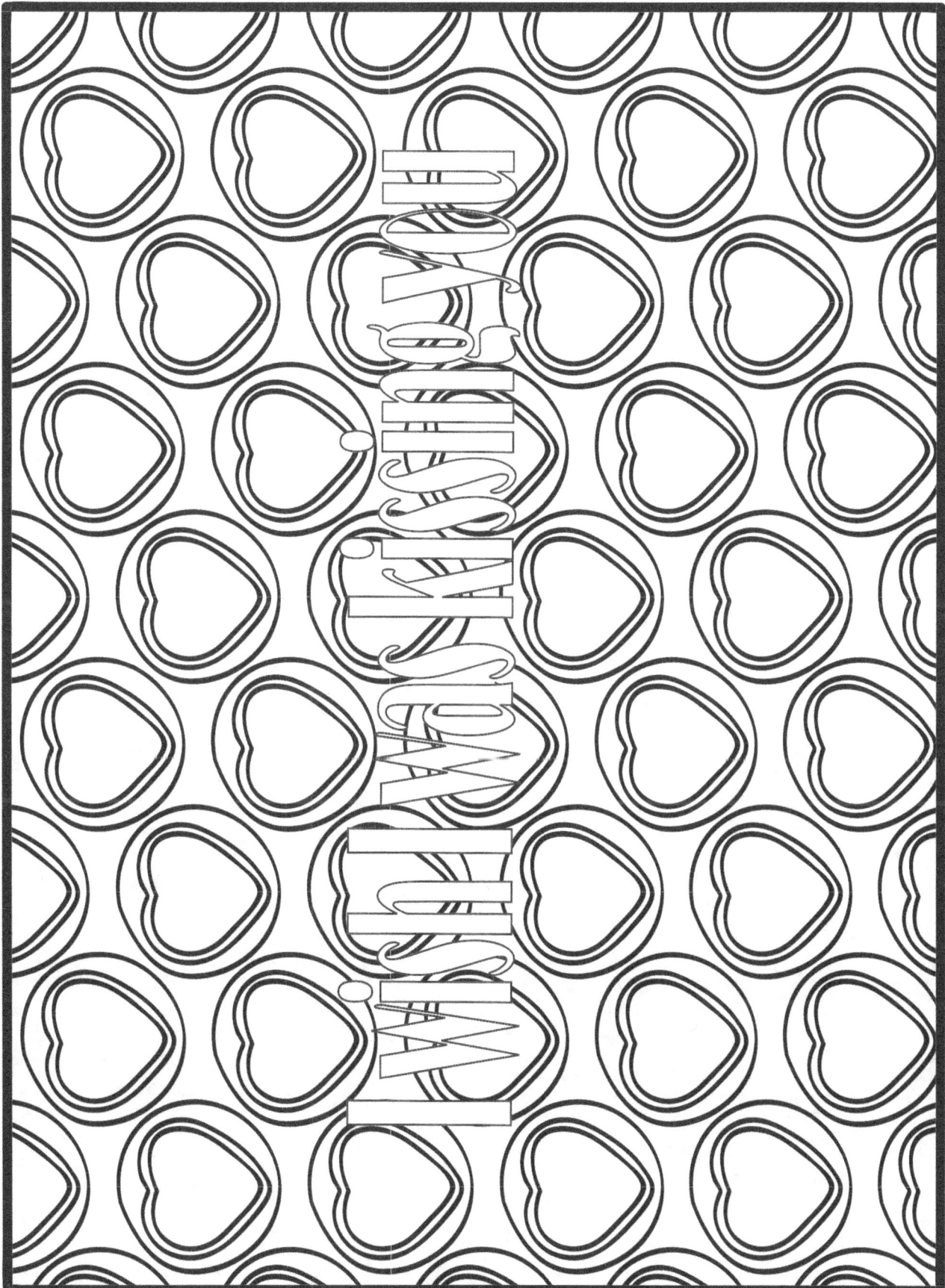

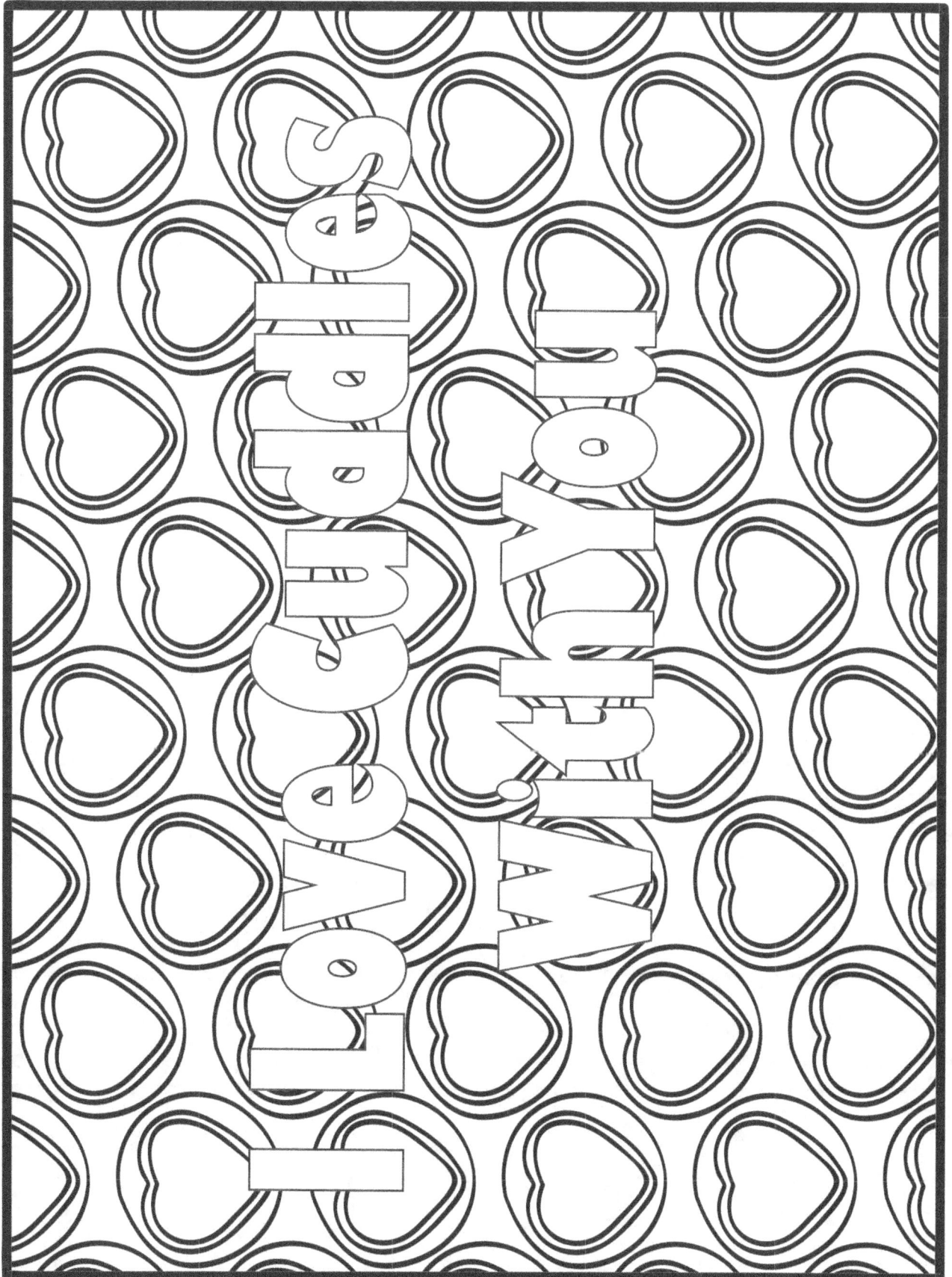

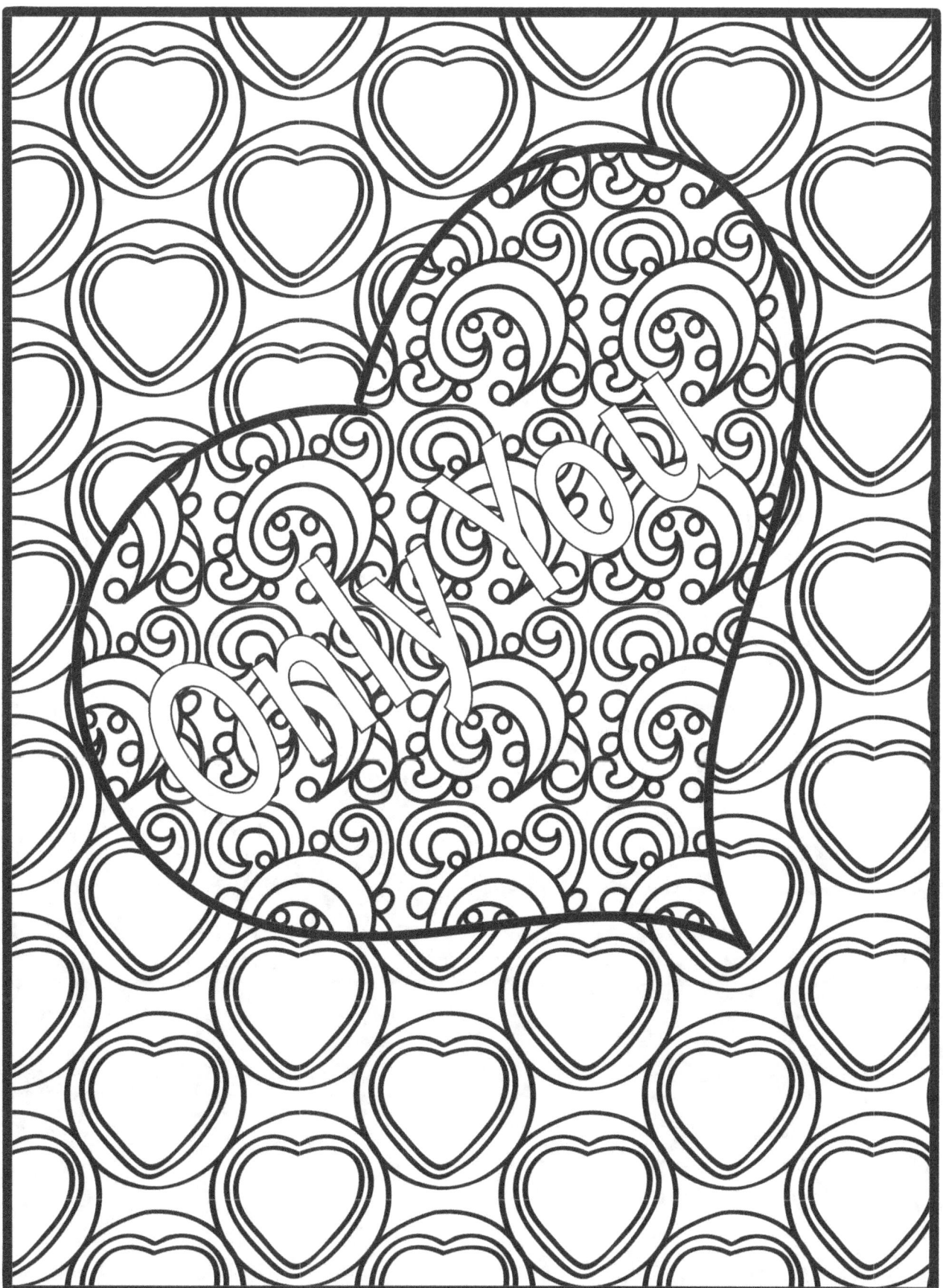

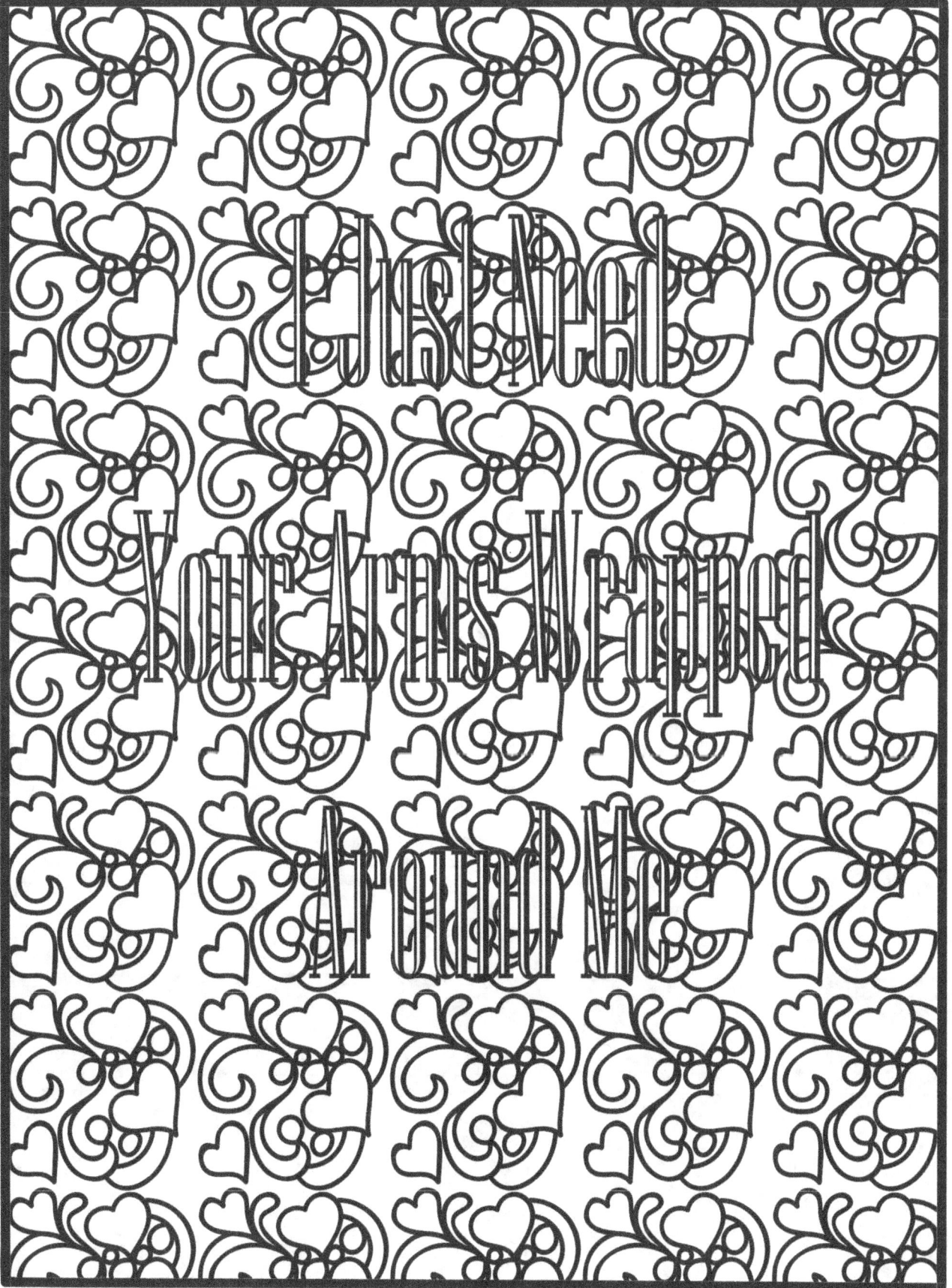

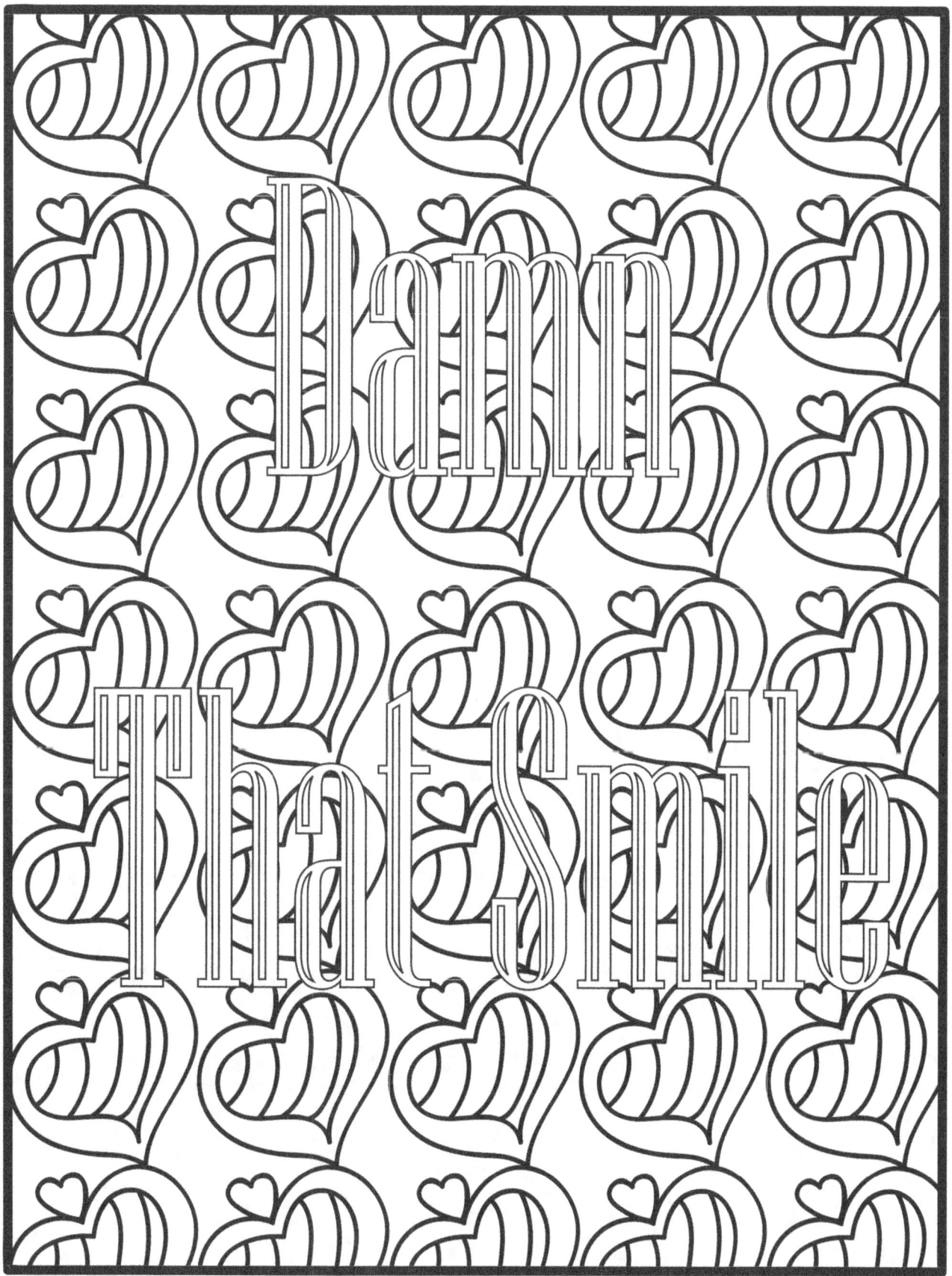

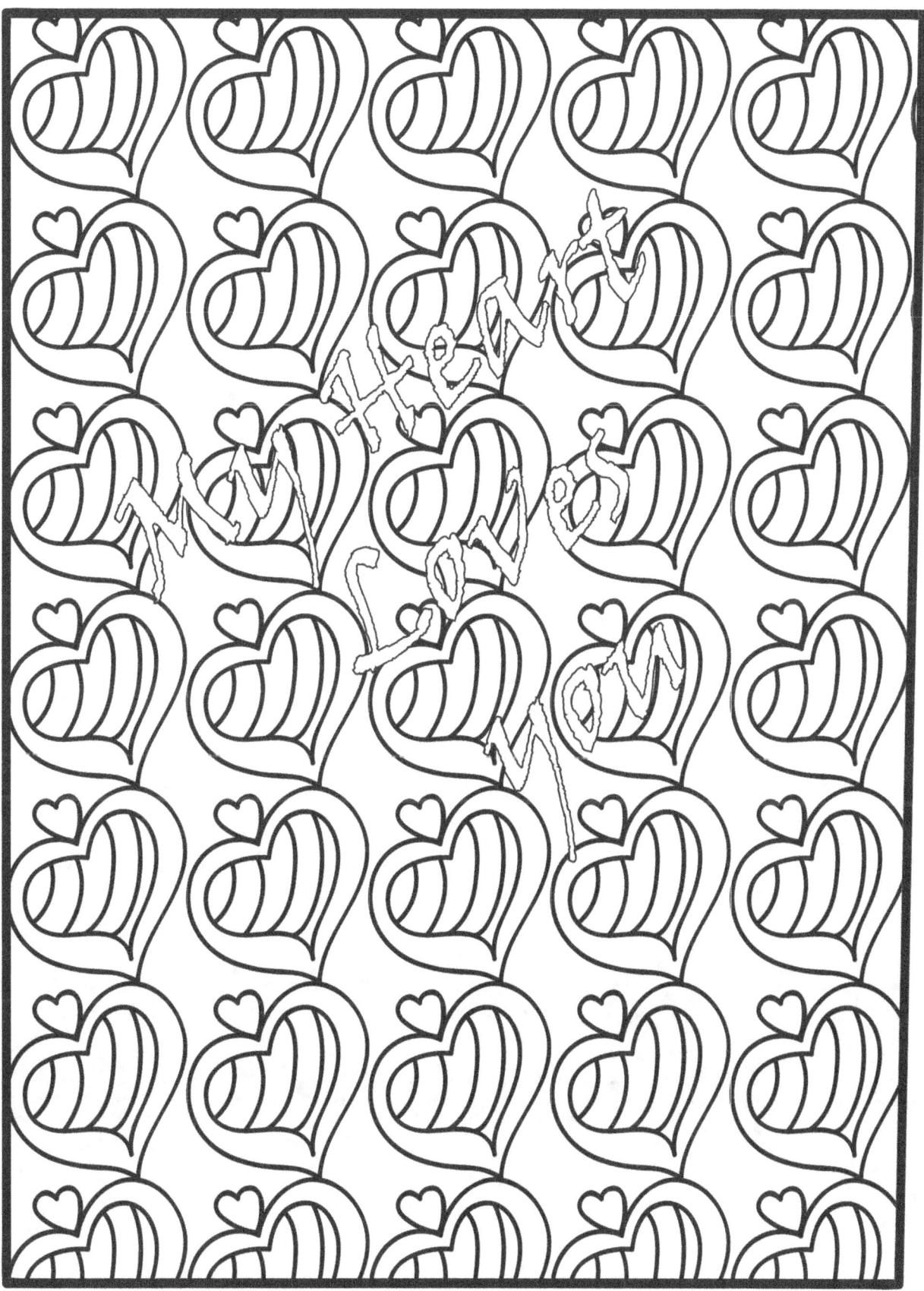

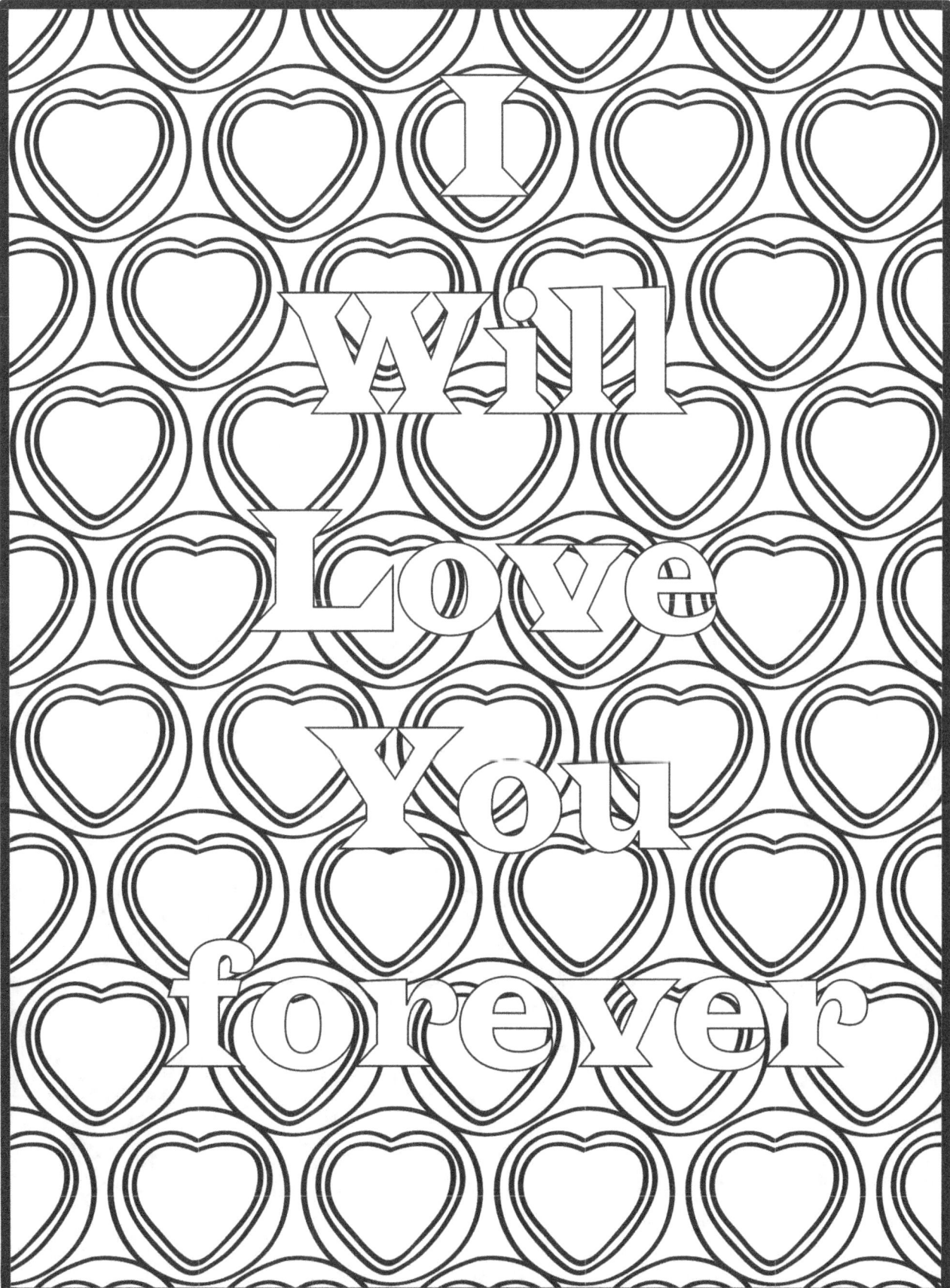

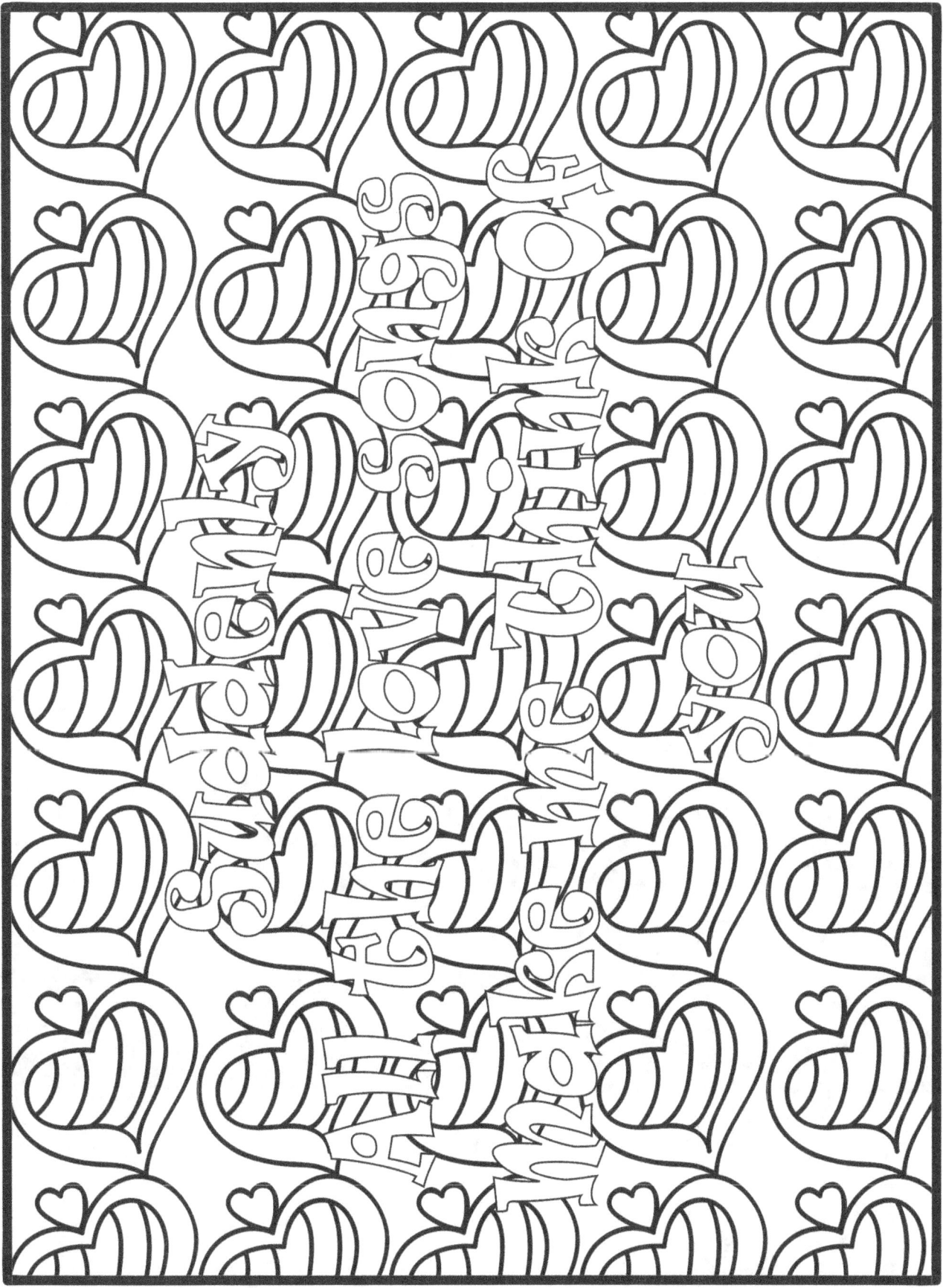

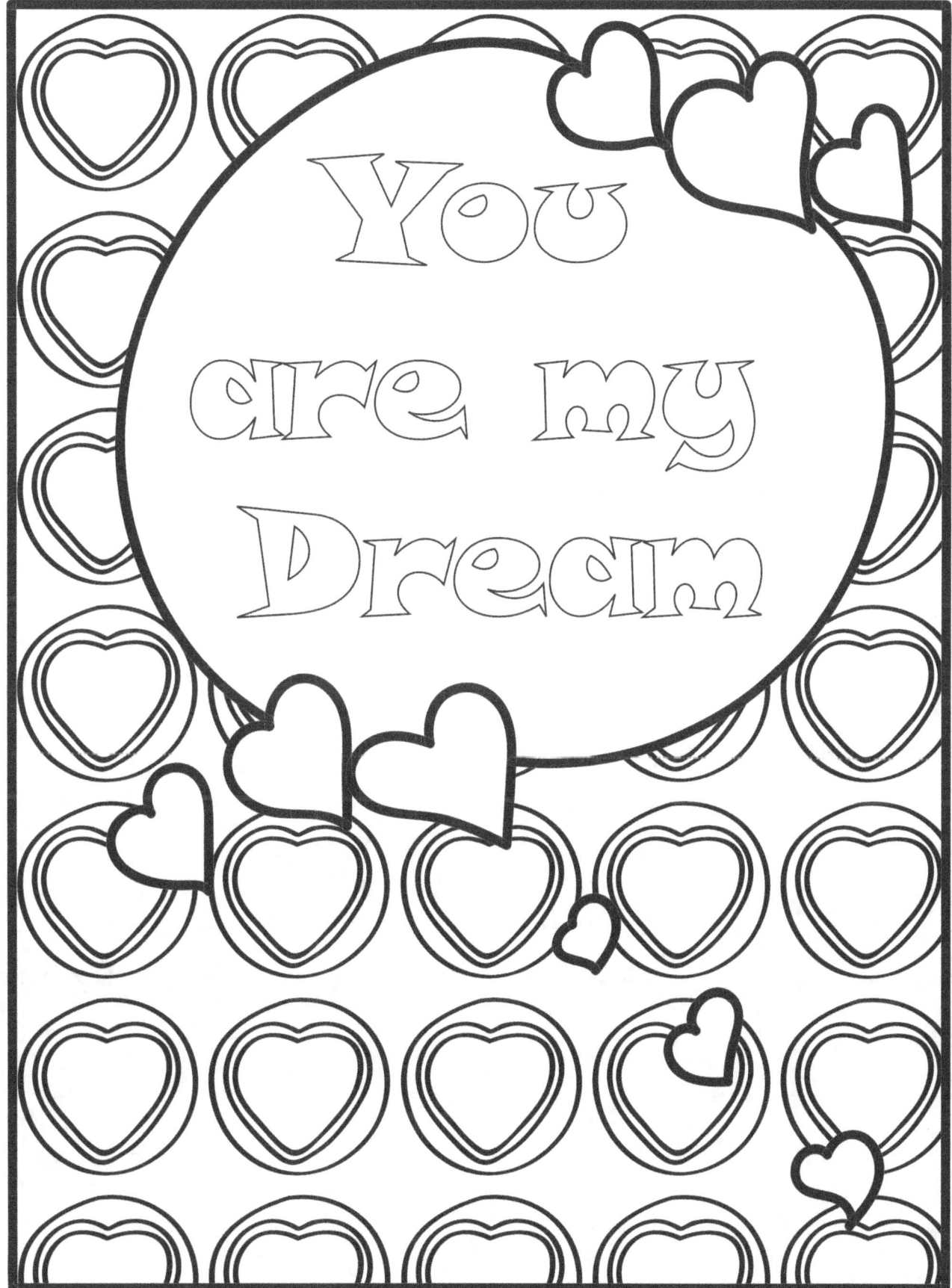

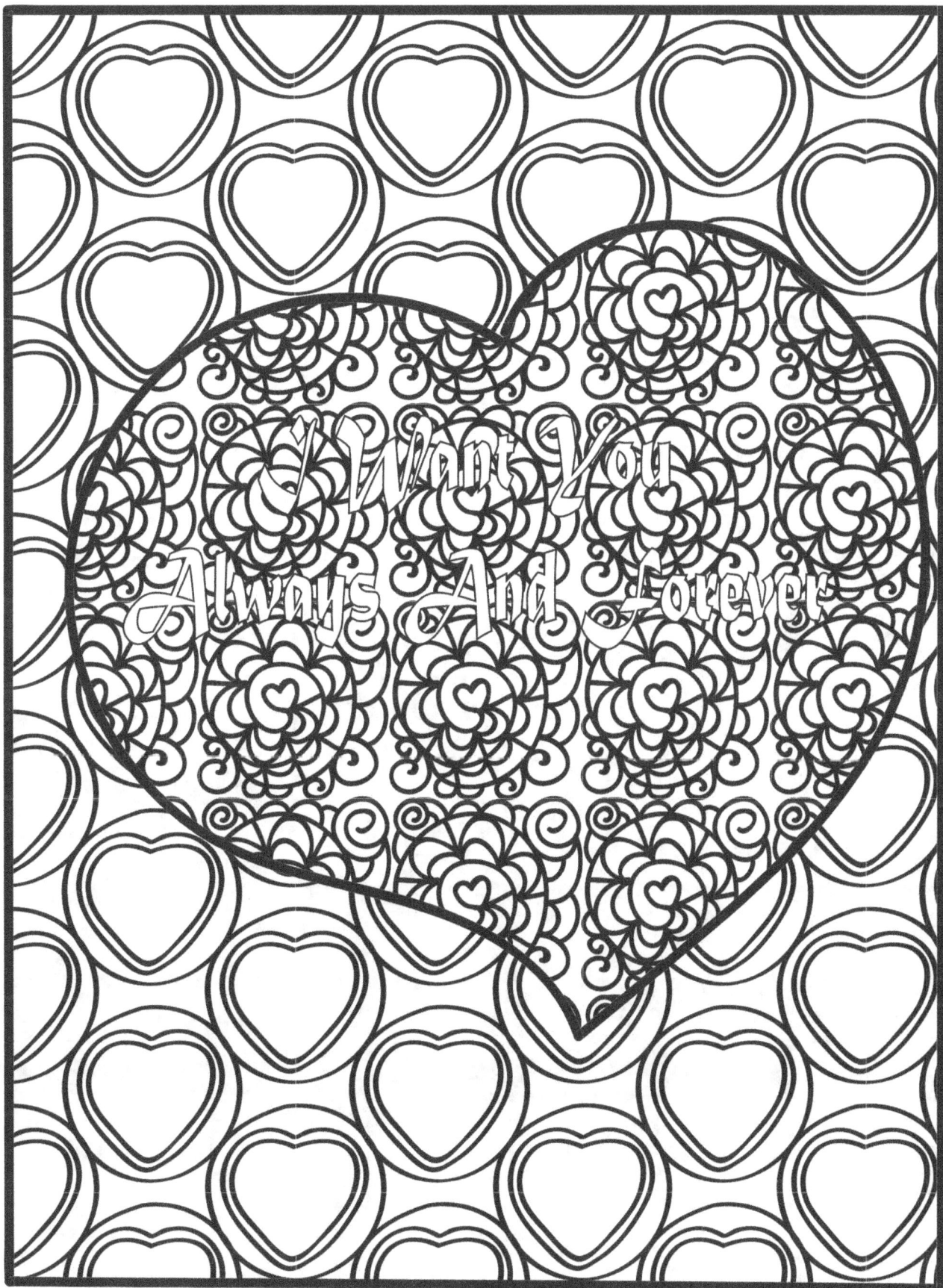

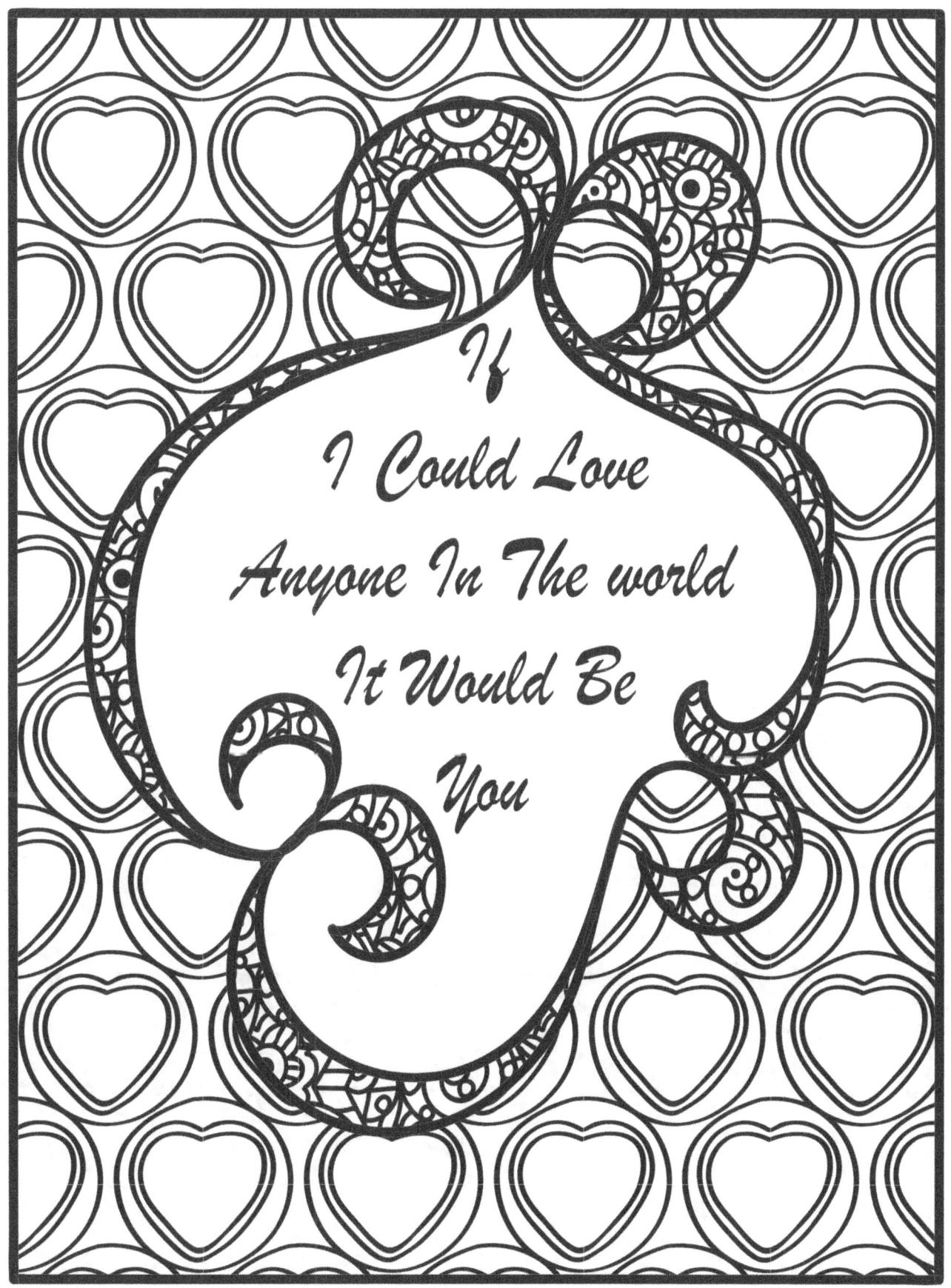

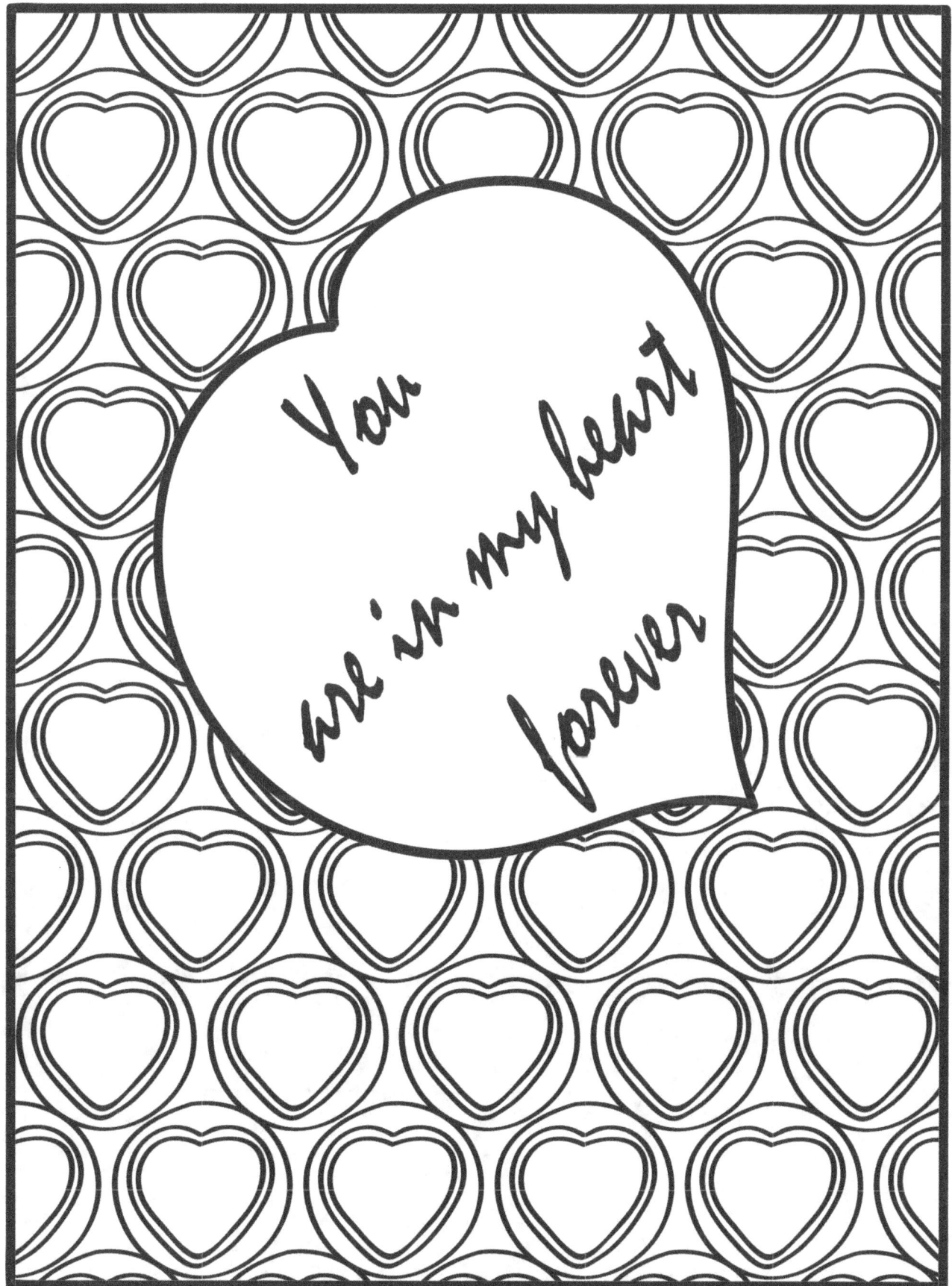

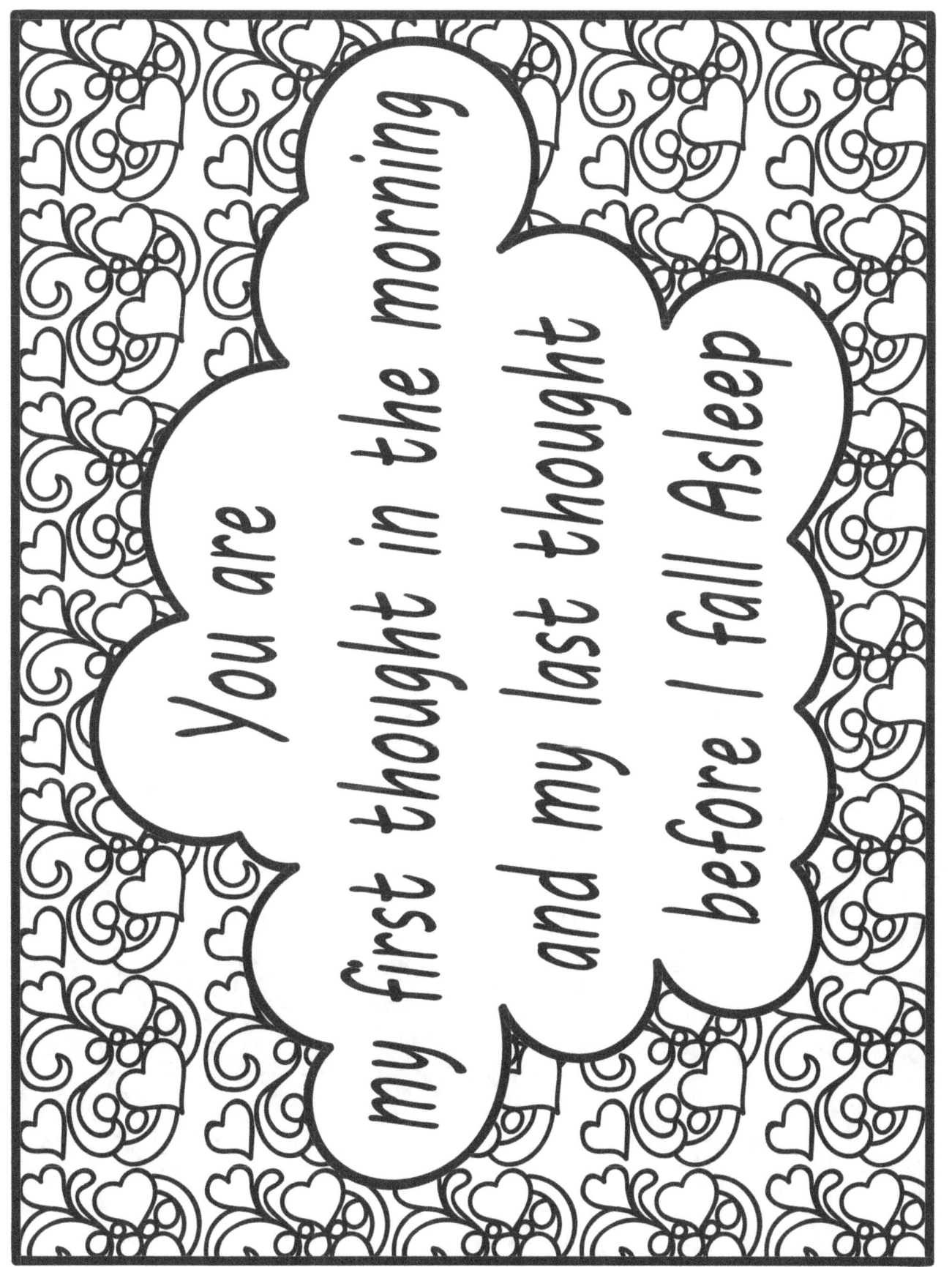

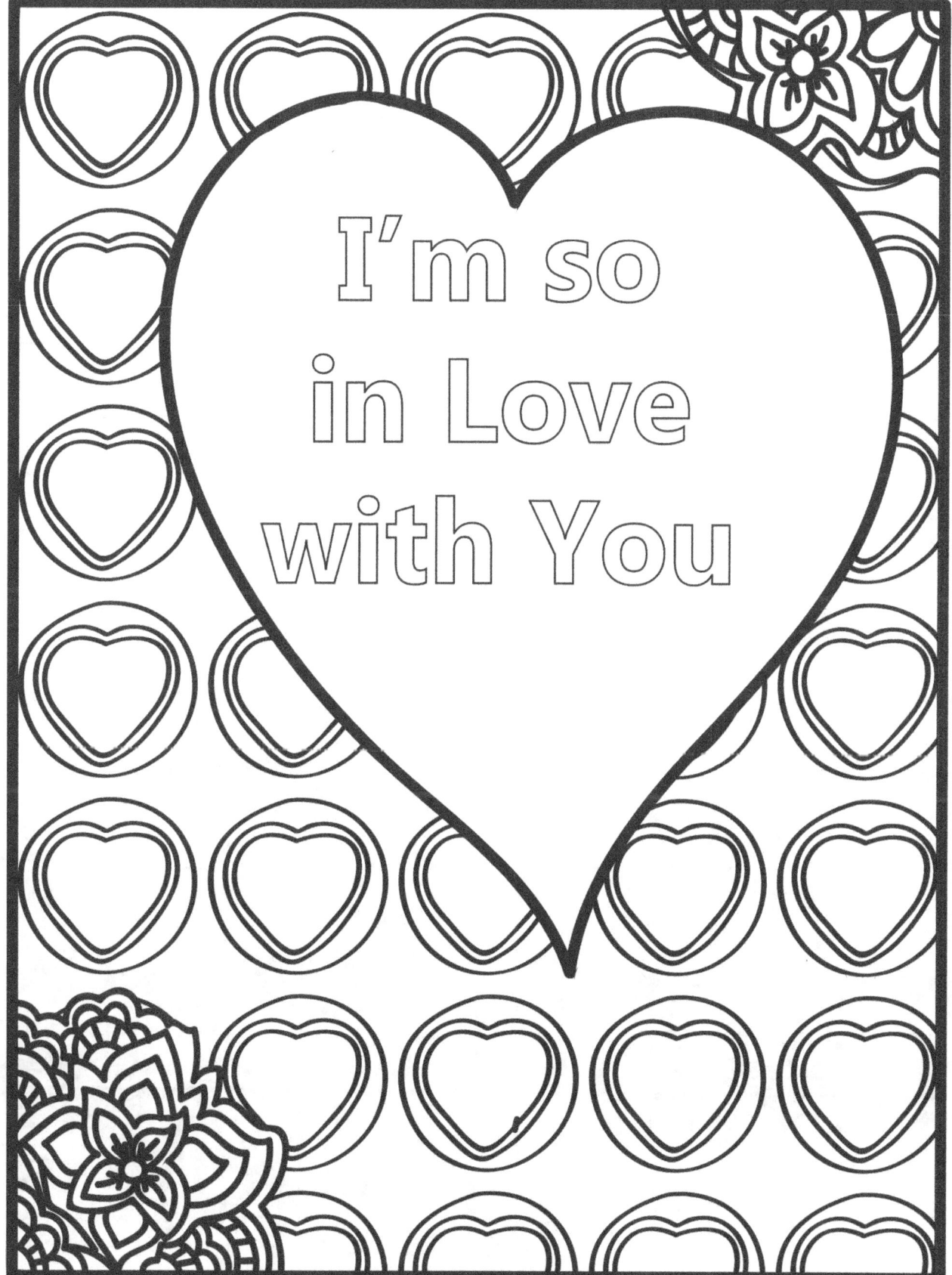

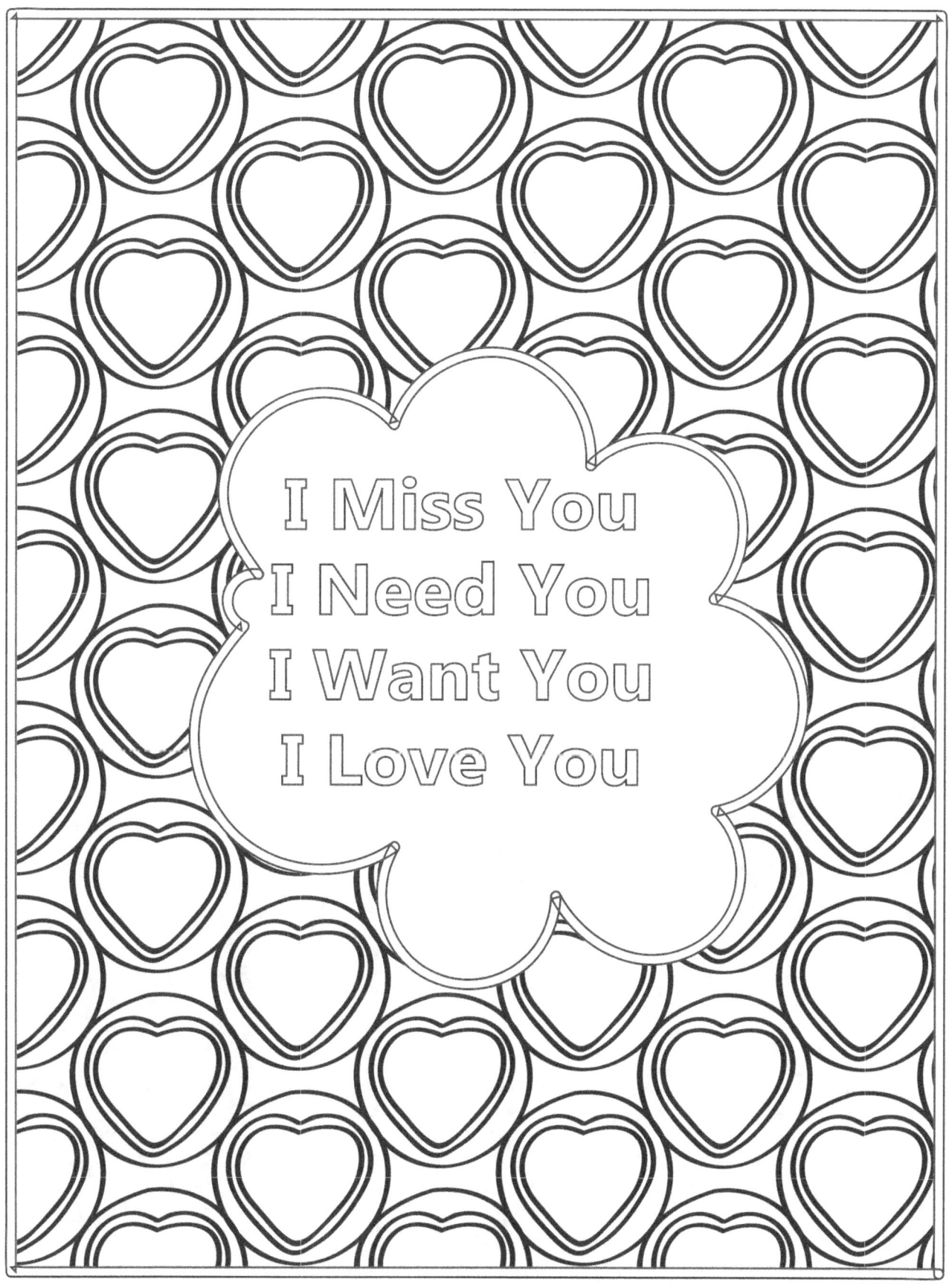

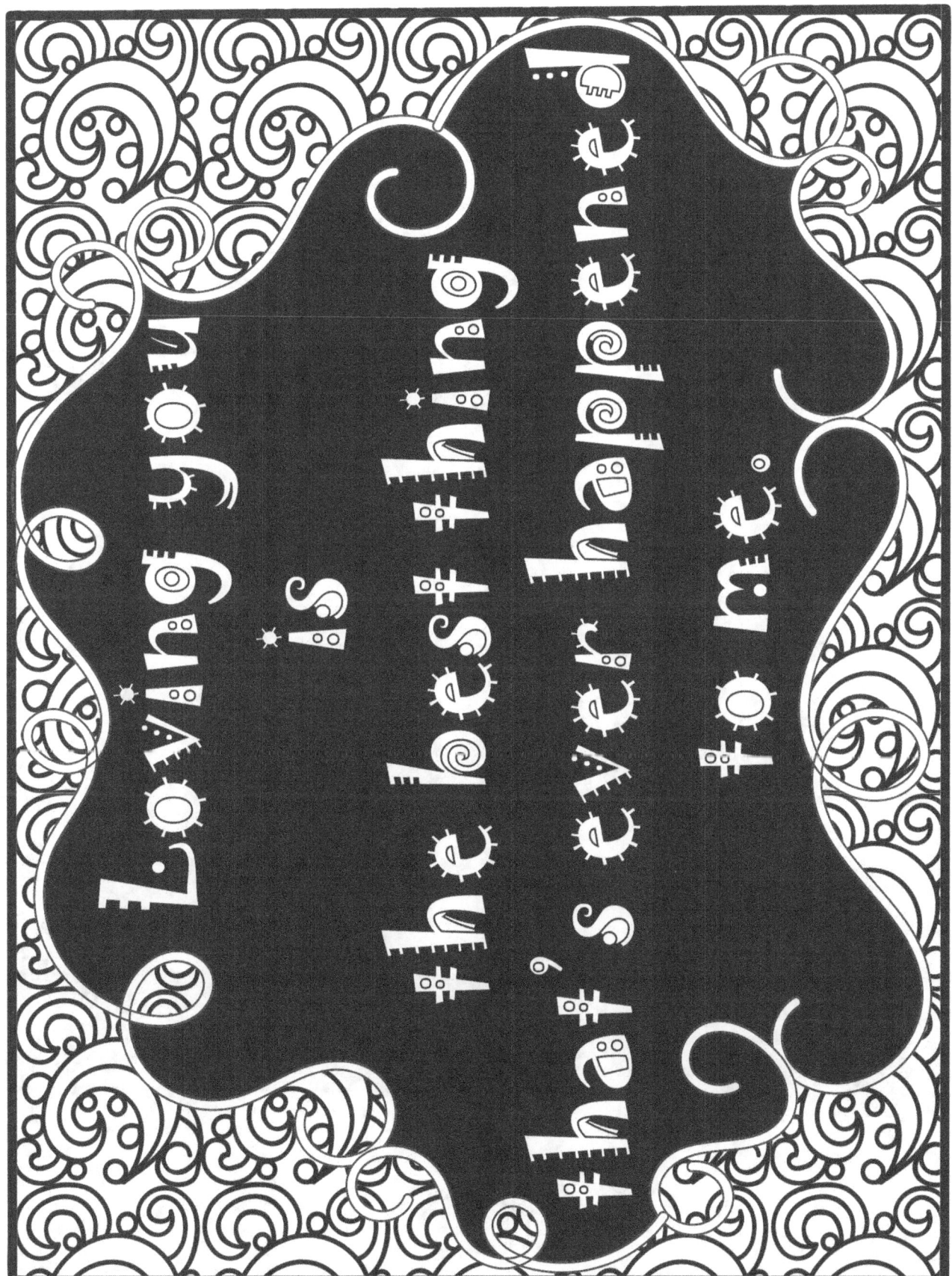

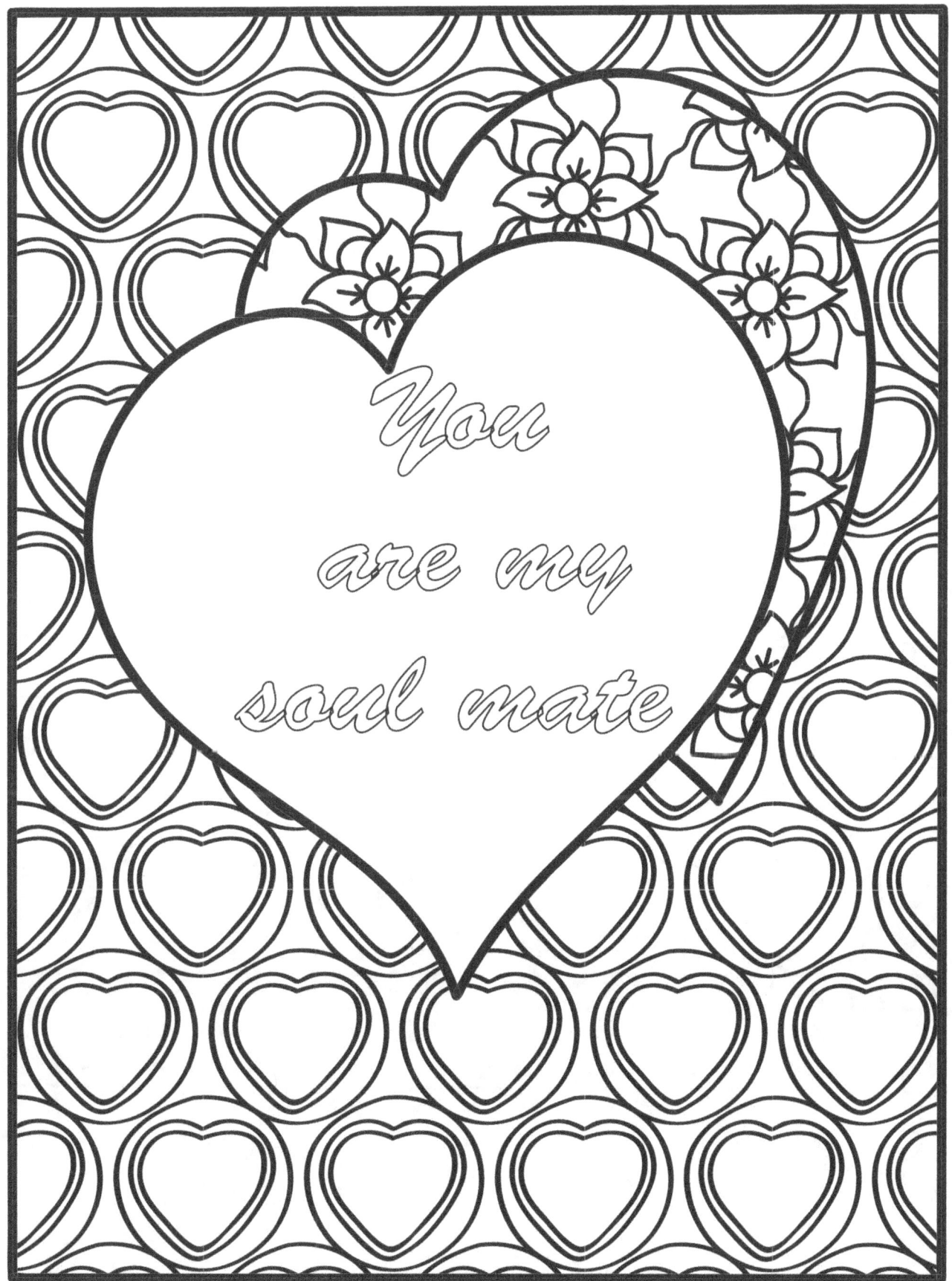

COLOR TEST PAGE

COLOR TEST PAGE

www.ingramcontent.com/pod-product-compliance
Lightning Source LLC
Chambersburg PA
CBHW080001230526
45470CB00008B/2825